YOU DON'T HAVE TO BE MAD TO WORK HERE...

Programmed by Roger Kilroy
Draughtsmanship by Ed McLachlan

J. M. Dent & Sons Ltd
London   Melbourne   Toronto

First published 1982

This book is set in 12/13½ point Lasercomp Times by
Northumberland Press Ltd, Gateshead
Printed in Great Britain
by Fletcher & Son Ltd, Norwich for
J.M. Dent & Sons Ltd
Aldine House, 33 Welbeck Street, London W1M 8LX

ISBN 0 460 04565 2

TO NOAH
The only man in history
who has been able to
float a limited company
when the rest of the world
was going into liquidation.

WELCOME

Painkillers can ruin your life – if you're a masochist.
This book should save yours – if you've got a job and
want to survive. It's a unique 'How to ...' book that
tells you everything you every wanted to know about life
at work but were too afraid/apathetic/inebriated to ask.

CONTENTS

HOW TO RECOGNISE THE WORKFORCE

The Chairman and his Wife

Don't have it off with your secretary. Have it off with someone else's secretary.

The Managing Director and his Secretary

The greatest labour-saving of today is... TOMORROW

I used to be indecisive, but now I'm not too sure.

I don't meet competition— I crush it!

The Sales Representative

Some are bent with toil and some get crooked trying to avoid it.

The Office Romeo

The Office Cleaner

The train arriving at Platforms 1, 2, 3, 4, and 5 is coming in sideways

DO YOUR BIT FOR UNEMPLOYMENT— GIVE SOMEONE YOUR JOB!

HOW TO BE A HAPPY COMMUTER

The contented commuter always has a song in his heart on his way to work – this song:

THE COMMUTER'S BARGING SONG

Jolly commuting weather
With snow up to your knees,
Trudging to the station,
There to sit and freeze.
Huddled up in the waiting-room,
With your bodies between your knees.
Huddled up in the waiting-room,
With your bodies between your knees.

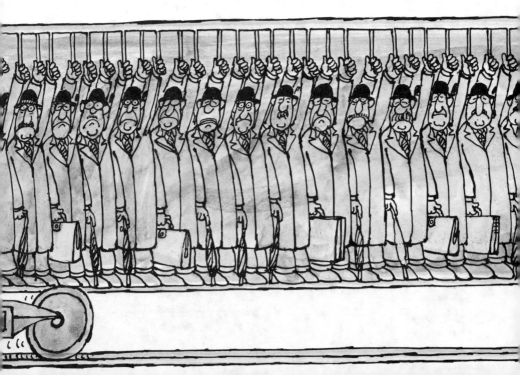

The Krauts may be more brainy,
The Wops may make more row,
But we struggle on together,
Stolid, resigned and cowed,
For nothing in life can ever
Be worse than the eight-ten from Slough.
For nothing in life can ever
Be worse than the eight-ten from Slough.

Others may take your places
Standing in the queue,
While we pant down the platform
Barging to get through.
And puce will be our faces
As we squeeze inside the tube,
And puce will be our faces
As we squeeze inside the tube.

NOTICE
Course in accounting for women.
For details please apply to Personnel Department
THERE IS NO ACCOUNTING FOR WOMEN

WHEN ALL IS SAID AND DONE, THERE'S MORE THAT'S SAID THAN DONE!

I wish I were what I was when I wished I were what I am.

HOW TO USE THE TELEPHONE

Apart from the kettle, the telephone is probably the most important piece of machinery in your office. As a link with the outside world, as a source of ever-growing information and as a means of keeping in touch with your friends for nothing, the office telephone is essential to business life.

There are two golden rules that will enable you to get the maximum benefit from your telephone;

(1) It is quite unnecessary to prolong any conversation over humdrum matters like contracts, delivery dates, complaints and orders. With only limited time at your disposal, the weather, the latest television programmes, the state of the family, must all take priority. In this day and age it's people that count, after all.

(2) As a public relations tool the telephone is second to none. More dates have been clinched over the phone than were ever made in a dance-hall. The tone of your voice, the excuse you make up for the liaison, the place from where you are phoning can all be conveniently disguised by the correct use of the telephone.

TELEPHONE CONVERSATIONS

As long as *you* are making the phone call, there should never be any trouble. Problems begin when people start telephoning you. Experience has taught that it is not possible to drink a cup of tea, or eat an office biscuit while conducting a telephone conversation. Under these circumstances you must get the caller to ring back.

As far as telephone language is concerned there are certain expressions that will be found of great value when answers and replies have to be given which may not be to the caller's liking. A list of the most common of these is given as guidance:

THE TRUTH	WHAT YOU SHOULD SAY
I don't want to take the call.	Hello ... hello ... hello (repeated after the caller has started speaking).
No.	O.K.; all right.
No.	I'd like to think about it.
Prelude to cutting off.	Will you hold the line please?
About to be dropped in the bin.	I'll give Mr ... your message.
He doesn't want to speak to you.	I'm sorry there's no reply.
He won't be in till 4.00.	I'm afraid Mr ... has just popped out for lunch
Perhaps you'll get the message.	I've tried to ring you several times.
Wednesday's golf day.	Mr ... has been called away to Head Office today.
He's knocking off his secretary.	Mr ... is busy dictating at the moment.
He's knocking off the other secretary.	Certainly, I'll connect you right away, Mrs ...

ever ever underestimate a woman unless you're discussing her age or her weight.

A SPECIALIST IS SOMEONE CALLED IN AT THE LAST MINUTE TO SHARE THE BLAME.

AN OPTIMIST IS A MAN WHO MARRIES HIS SECRETARY WITH THE IDEA THAT HE'LL BE ABLE TO CARRY ON DICTATING TO HER!

A friend in need is a friend to avoid.

What some in this office lack in intelligence, they more than make up in stupidity.

HOW TO USE THE DICTATING MACHINE

1. The start of the letter will be indicated by the words: 'Oh hell, the ****ing battery's run down again.'

2. Paragraphs will be indicated by a sneeze.

3. Full stops, question marks, colons, semi-colons, dashes and exclamation marks can be ignored unless an audible yawn is heard.

4. Commas will occur at the end of each breath. The dictator need only dictate for the duration of each breath. Where he or she pauses, a comma should be entered.

5. Parenthesis will be indicated by the inclusion of any word which is unprintable either here, or in any letter.

6. The apostrophe will be indicated by a raising of the voice; the thumping of the desk; the sound of smashing in the background.

7. Instructions for headings will precede the words of the heading, e.g. 'Let's try and get it right this time shall we, cloth-ears? – Monthly Sales Prospective Number 8.'

8. The twenty-four hour clock shall be dictated as spoken, e.g. 16.45, or when Noddy is pointing at 9 and Biggy Ears is pointing at 4.

9. Abbreviations will be dictated to show whether stops are required or not, e.g. 'Norwich – capitals: N stop O stop R stop W stop I stop C stop H stop – Nickers Off Ready When I Come Home – Yes, Miss.... "Nickers" should be spelt with a K but I'm employing poetic licence – amongst other things.'

Of course, if your company doesn't run to dictating machines, you'll simply have to dictate to your secretary in person ...

'O.K. – got another pencil? Last one ...
Dear Sir,
Right. What can I tell the boring old fart. Begin – In answer to your enquiry of the eighth last I am surprised to learn that you have been experiencing difficulties with your recent purchase. As you know the lorry you bought from us had always given perfect satisfaction until its sale. We had to flog it quick before the engine dropped out and the rear diff went for a burton; the silly bugger coughed up nine hundred quid for it. New paragraph.

As you know, we take care in inspecting all of our used vehicles thoroughly before parting with them. Your lorry was in first-class condition when it left our workshops. That's a stunning outfit you've got on. New, isn't it? New paragraph.

Might I respectfully suggest that your driver might be at fault? Four miles to the gallon certainly is very poor mileage for a vehicle such as yours. Four gallons to the mile is what we were getting from it down hill at the end. You know I'd never noticed that dimple there, but then we don't get many secretaries like you in this firm. However, as we always endeavour to provide a comprehensive back-up service to all of our customers, perhaps you would care to bring the vehicle round to us so that one of our expert mechanics can make any necessary adjustments to the engine. That should shut him up. Post it second class.

Yours sincerely,
Just sign it yourself. Well, what about that lunch ...'

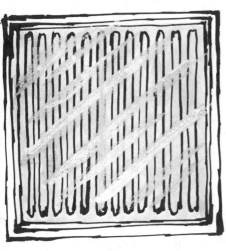

OUT TO LUNCH
-IF NOT BACK
BY FIVE OUT
TO DINNER ALSO

Owing to the fuel
crisis, officials
are advised to take
advantage of their
secretaries between
12 p.m. and 2 p.m.

SHE WAS ONL
THE MORSE
CODE OPERATO
DAUGHTER, BU
SHE DID IT DID
DID DID DID IT

29

HOW TO HANDLE YOUR CORRESPONDENCE

The best business letters are true works of literature. Here are some genuine examples to help inspire you ...

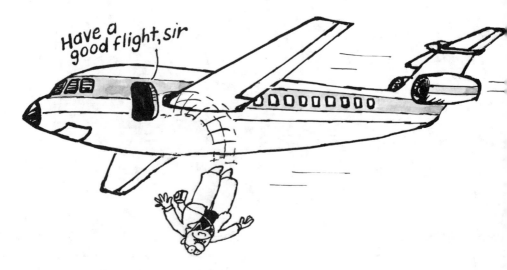

Have a good flight, sir

Dear Sir,
    With reference to our letter re Majorca tour, the flight you mention is completely booked, but we will inform you immediately someone falls out, as usually happens.

Dear Madam,
    With reference to your blue raincoat, our manufacturers have given the garment in question a thorough testing, and find that it is absolutely waterproof. If you will wear it on a dry day, and then take it off and examine it, you will see that our statement is correct.

Dear Madam,
    In reply to your letter, we are very sorry for the delay in sending the house-coat, but the tremendous demand for these has denuded our stock. We are, however, expecting further delay in a day or so.

Sir,

For the case that your electric light should fail we beg to send you enclosed a postcard which please send us at once when you find your light out. The company will then send you another postcard.

Yours truly,

Manager, Siam Electricity Co. Ltd.

Dear Sir stroke Madam,

Would you please try your telephone now, and if you are unable to use it would you please report the difficulty by dialling 151.

Dear Member,

This rule is included as a concession solely to cover the position of members who died whilst they were away on sick leave at reduced rates. It was contemplated that they would pay up any arrears on return to duty.

Dear Colleagues,

Since the former secretary had left the area and the former minutes could not be found, it was moved, seconded and carried that the minutes of the last meeting be adopted, as they would have been read had they been found.

Dear Customer,

The British firm Digitronics Ltd. has changed its name to Digitronix Ltd, to avoid confusion with a US firm with a similar sounding name.

Dear Sir/Madam,

You have been served with your cactus by our Rainwear Staff. We have unfortunately been unable to teach our computer the difference between an umbrella and a cactus. Therefore, on your next monthly statement, your cactus will be described as an umbrella.

Dear Subscriber,

If you bought our course: *How to fly in six easy lessons*, we apologize for any inconvenience caused by our failure to include the last chapter, titled: *How to land your plane safely*. Send us your name and address and we will forward it to you post haste.

Dear Sir,

The title of the film *Plink Plonk Plink* (F52377), registered on 7 June, 1967, has been corrected to read *Plink Plunk Plink*.

Sir,

It is regretted that it was not possible to send the enclosed forms to you before the date by which, had you received them, you would be required to forward completed copies to this office.

BE WARNED: If you don't send out the right kind of letter, you won't get the right kind of reply ... This letter was sent by an Australian stamp collector to his supplier:

Sir,

I am intensely dissatisfied with your organization and shall recommend it to the Russians as a prime nuclear target.

You are confused as to what the problem is. Let me explain while I have some workable sanity left:
(1) I receive a set of covers in due order.
(2) I send off my payment in due order.
(3) 60 to 90 days later I get a past due notice.
(4) I panic.
(5) I check my records and find that I have paid in due order and therefore your notice is all wrong.
(6) This has happened with every issue since May '77.
(7) I gnash my teeth, pull my hair and rend my garments.
(8) I complain but nobody listens.

Now I find that I have received and paid for 25 sets or $125 worth. Set #25 is not accounted for in your letter. I sent you payment for that one way back in ancient times, so you should have a record of it, but I just have the absolute feeling that I will soon be receiving a past due notice for it.

I have no choice therefore but to visit upon you my own particular divine wrath and *cancel my subscription.*

Executive - one who can take a two-hour lunch-break any day of the week without being missed.

AT UNION CONFERENCES, FACTIONS SPEAK LOUDER THAN WORDS.

GONE TO LUNCH

DIGESTING LUNCH

MY boss has boots so shiny I can see my face in them.

IF TIME IS MONEY, WE'RE ALL LIVING BEYOND OUR MEANS

A workers rights are those which belong to him which he can't have.

The only person to get everything done by Friday was Robinson Crusoe!

HOW TO MAKE YOUR EXCUSES

A.M.
'He hasn't come in yet.'
'I expect him in any minute.'
'He just sent word in he'd be a little late.'
'He's been in, but he went out again.'
'He's gone to lunch.'

P.M.

'I expect him in any minute.'

'He hasn't come back yet. Can I take a message?'

'He's somewhere in the building. His coat is here.'

'Yes, he was in, but he went out again.'

'I don't know whether he'll be back or not.'

'No, he's gone for the day.'

Don't vote Labour— vote TGWU and cut out the middleman.

WHEN IT COMES TO GIVING THIS FIRM STOPS AT NOTHING!

When you're right in this office, no one remembers. When you're wrong, no one forgets!

People speak about unemployment as if work was a four-letter word.

WHY WASTE TIME WORKING EIGHT HOURS A DAY JUST TO BECOME THE BOSS AND WORK TWELVE HOURS A DAY.

He who hesitates is bossed!

HOW TO COMMUNICATE BY NUMBERS

If you need an excuse, just think of a number ...

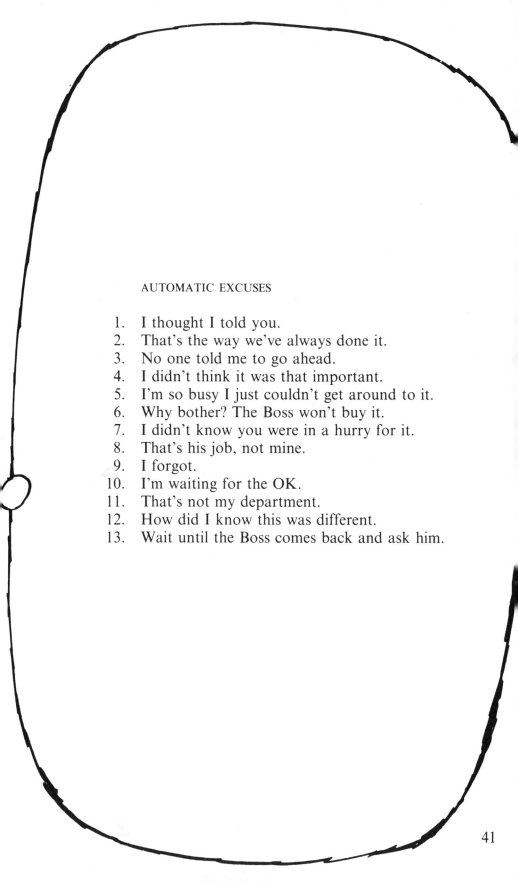

AUTOMATIC EXCUSES

1. I thought I told you.
2. That's the way we've always done it.
3. No one told me to go ahead.
4. I didn't think it was that important.
5. I'm so busy I just couldn't get around to it.
6. Why bother? The Boss won't buy it.
7. I didn't know you were in a hurry for it.
8. That's his job, not mine.
9. I forgot.
10. I'm waiting for the OK.
11. That's not my department.
12. How did I know this was different.
13. Wait until the Boss comes back and ask him.

In the interests of efficiency and harmonious industrial relations the management have installed a computer to deal with all internal dialogue. Employees are requested to express their views by number from now on.

1. It's a return to the 1920s.
2. We've been doing it this way for forty years.
3. This company is different.
4. Maybe, but we're not in Japan, are we.
5. Look what happened to Chrysler.
6. We've never done it before.
7. We don't have the facilities.
8. Not until our previous demands are met.
9. It won't work in a small company.
10. It won't work in a large company.
11. It won't work in this company.
12. Our brothers fought for forty years to stop it.
13. Why change when it's working OK?
14. Not now you've done away with our differentials.
15. What about our differentials?
16. What's the catch?
17. We don't have the manpower.
18. You can't teach an old dog new tricks.
19. The lads will never buy it.
20. Who do you think you are – Sir Michael Edwardes?
21. It's against union policy.
22. With three million unemployed you must be joking.
23. You may be able to con the other lads, but we'll be out.
24. Don't think you'd win if it went to arbitration.
25. With this equipment, you must be kidding.
26. This is the thin end of the wedge.
27. We're doing all right as it is.
28. The union's not ready for it.
29. It's too much trouble to change.

30. It needs sleeping on.
31. The night shift won't like it.
32. It's not our problem.
33. It's not my job.
34. It won't work in this section.
35. It's never been done in this firm.
36. They'd call us blacklegs.
37. You want all that and a productivity agreement, too?
38. If it works there, let them keep it.
39. It can't be done.
40. So what.
41. Not until we get the thirty-five hour week.
42. The canteen staff say it can't be done.
43. You'll have to agree with the other branches first.
44. It'll make a mockery of the negotiation procedure.
45. What's it worth?
46. This isn't Poland.
47. It'll have to go to the executive.
48. And who's to say you're right anyway?
49. Over my dead body.
50. **** ***!

THE WORLD IS FULL
OF SURPRISES – FEW OF THEM
ARE PLEASANT – TRY WORKING HER

God might have created the world
in six days, but he didnt have to
do it in triplicate !!!

Going to a psychiatrist
didn't cure my drink proble
–I kept falling off the couch.

MOST OF US WOULD ENJOY THE DAY
MORE IF IT STARTED LATER !

Doing a good job here is
like wetting yourself in
a dark suit ; you get a
warm feeling...
...but nobody notices.

Credit must be given to the worker with a large family —he can't live without it!

HOW TO SAVE ENERGY AND IMPROVE EFFICIENC

ENERGY — EXPENDITURE AND ECONOMIES

In the light of government directives to save energy the
Board has undertaken an exhaustive survey of the stress
factors born by employees in the course of their work. The
following statistics indicate the broad outlines of the
findings.

The figures relate to the number of calories expended in
any given activity in any given period of sixty minutes
(1 hour):

Running fast	975
Running moderately fast	850
Climbing stairs at 2.5 km/h	620
Walking at 6.5 km/h	492
Driving car	168
Standing	118
Sitting and writing	114
Sitting	108
Lying in bed	60

As a result of this survey the Board has concluded that:

(a) All employees should endeavour to travel to work by car, ideally with someone else driving.
(b) They should avoid using the stairs whenever possible.
(c) The firm should move into brand-new single-storey offices.
(d) Offices will be equipped with beds to replace the stress-intensive furniture currently in use.
(e) The Sports Club be disbanded forthwith.
(f) All correspondence will be sent verbally with immediate effect.

It is hoped that all employees will do their utmost to follow these simple instructions as part of our efforts to respond to the government's initiative to curb energy waste.

To be inspired by a real efficiency expert in action, read his report on a concert given recently at London's Royal Festival Hall ...

During much of the work period, the four oboe players had nothing to do. Their numbers should be reduced and their work should be distributed more evenly throughout the work period, so eliminating peaks of activity.

The twelve violin players were all playing identical notes. This is unnecessary duplication. This section should be drastically pruned. If the resultant cuts lead to a reduction in sound, electronic apparatus will more than make up for the loss in manpower.

Considerable time was spent in the playing of demi-semi-quavers; this seems to be an unnecessary refinement. It is recommended, therefore, that all notes be rounded up to the nearest semi-quaver. If this practice was adopted, it would make it possible to employ trainees and lower-grade operatives more extensively.

Similarly there is excessive repetition of many musical passages. There is wide scope for modification and reduction here. Little contribution is made by repeating on the woodwind a passage that has already been dealt with thoroughly by the strings. If all such redundant passages were eliminated, it is estimated that the whole work period, currently two hours, could be reduced to twenty minutes, which would also obviate the need for an interval.

The conductor has been consulted about these recommendations and is generally in agreement with them, though the opinion was expressed that there might be some falling off in box-office receipts. If this indeed proves to be the case, it should be possible to close sections of the auditorium entirely. This would result in additional savings in overhead expenses, heating, lighting, attendance, etc. And if the worst came to the worst, the entire programme could be shut down and the public could attend a similar work period at the Albert Hall instead.

If you can't get your work done in twenty-four hours, work nights.

THIS WAY UP
IF YOU WANT TO SEE
A HEALTHY PROFIT.

Never fall into the trap of confusing motion with progress.

A 5-day week is just a 4-day week that takes a little longer to get through

And on the fifth day God saw that it was good...and rested.

The reason for the rush is the delay, and the reason for the delay is the rush!

IF IT LOOKS EASY, IT'S GOING TO BE HARD. IF IT LOOKS HARD, IT'S GOING TO BE DAMN'NEAR IMPOSSIBLE

Bees are never as busy as they sound – they just don't know how to buzz slower.

ZZZZZZ

ZZZZ

The first 90% of the task takes 10% of the time and the last 10% takes 90% of the time.

HOW TO LIVE WITH A COMPUTER

Learn the rules of the game ...

UTZ'S LAW OF COMPUTER PROGRAMMING

(1) Any given programme, when running, is obsolete.
(2) Any given programme costs more and takes longer.
(3) If a programme is useful, it will have to be changed.
(4) Any given programme will expand to fill all available memory.
(5) If a programme is useless, it will be documented.
(6) The value of a programme is proportional to the volume of its output.
(7) Programme complexity grows until it exceeds the capability of the programmer who must maintain it.
(8) Make it possible for programmers to write programmes in English, and you will find that programmers cannot write English.

LANDAU'S PROGRAMMING PARADOXES

(1) The world's best programmer has to be someone.
(2) The more humanlike a computer becomes, the less it spends time computing and the more it spends time doing more humanlike work.
(3) A software committee of one is limited by its own horizon and will specify software only that far.
(4) When the system programmers declare the system works, it has worked and will work again some day.

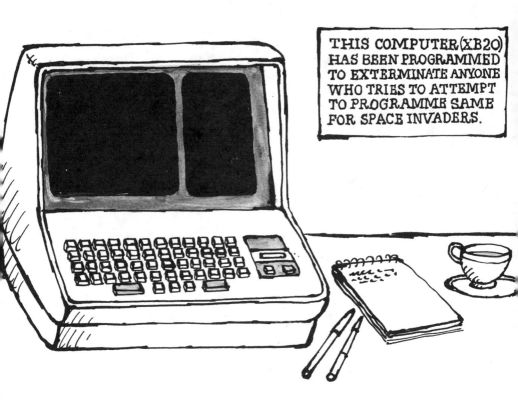

THIS COMPUTER (XB20) HAS BEEN PROGRAMMED TO EXTERMINATE ANYONE WHO TRIES TO ATTEMPT TO PROGRAMME SAME FOR SPACE INVADERS.

DON'T WORRY ABOUT COMPUTERS.
IF THEY GET TOO POWERFUL, JUS
ORGANISE THEM INTO COMMITTEES.

Computerised gossip
is just micro-chip-chat.

IF GOD HAD MEANT US TO GO
METRIC, WHY DID HE GIVE
JESUS TWELVE DISCIPLES?

The cause of problems
are solutions!

Efficiency is just a highly developed form of laziness.

ALL THE WORLD'S AN ANALOG STAGE, AND DIGITAL CIRCUITS PLAY ONLY BIT PARTS.

The length of any meeting rises with the square of the number of people present.

USE YOUR HEAD — IT'S THE LITTLE THINGS THAT COUNT!

HOW TO RUN THE PERSONNEL DEPARTMENT

To run a personnel department successfully you have got to be able to recognise the true qualities and potential of prospective employees ...

	POTENTIAL	
	OUTSTANDING	HIGHLY SATISFACTORY
OVERALL ABILITY	Leaps tall buildings with a single bound	Needs running start to jump tall building
TIMELINESS	Faster than speeding bullet	Only as fast as speeding bullet
INITIATIVE	Stronger than locomotive	Stronger than bull elephant
ADAPTABILITY	Walks on water consistently	Only walks on water in emergencies
COMMUNICATION	Talks with God	Talks with angels
RELATIONSHIP	Belongs in general management	Belongs in executive ranks
PLANNING	Too bright to worry	Worries about future

QUALITIES

SATISFACTORY	LESS SATISFACTORY	UNSATISFACTORY
Can only leap small buildings	Crashes into buildings	Cannot recognize buildings
Somewhat slower than bullet	Can only shoot bullets	Wounds self with bullets
Stronger than bull	Shoots bull	Smells like bull
Washes with water	Drinks water	Passes water in emergencies
Talks to self	Argues with self	Loses those arguments
Belongs in rank and file	Belongs behind broom	Belongs with competitor
Worries about present	Worries about past	Too thick to worry

You also need to master the precise language of the seasoned personnel officer ...

CONFIDENTIAL

In line with the new plans for reorganizing the Personnel Department the following phrases are to be employed when completing staff reports. These reports are to remain 'open'. However, in the interests of efficiency the following meanings will be attached to each one:

Keen sense of humour	Tells endless strings of dirty jokes – idle.
Zealous attitude	Opinionated.
Unlimited potential	Will stay with us until retirement.
Tactful in dealings with superiors	Knows when to keep his/her mouth shut.
Maintains professional attitude	A snob.
Conscientious and careful	Easily intimidated.
Stern disciplinarian	A right sod.
Slightly below average	Thick as two short planks.
Forceful and aggressive	Argumentative.
Character above reproach	We haven't caught up with him/her yet.
Indifferent to instruction	Knows more than we do.
Active socially	Drinks heavily.
Average	Not too bright.
Gets along extremely well with subordinates and superiors alike	Chicken.
Willing to spend extra hours in the office	Wretched home life.
Strong adherence to principles	Pig-headed.
Quick thinking	Never short of a plausible excuse for errors.

Expresses himself/herself well	Speaks English.
Approaches difficult problems logically	Gets someone else to carry the can.
A keen analyst	Thoroughly confused.
Of great value to the company	Turns in work on time.
Never misses any advantage to progress	Buys drinks for superiors.
Meticulous attention to detail	Can't see the wood for the trees.
Judgement is usually sound	Lucky.
Not a 'desk' man	No higher education.
Demonstrates qualities of leadership	Loud mouth.

When assessing staff for possible promotion you may find it helpful to use this form ...

STAFF ASSESSMENT

Employee's Name   Department

Assessed by   Date

Put cross through appropriate rating in each case:

MIEN   Low   High
(a) Gestures:—V-signs and their frequency;   1 2 3 4 5 6
    variety of faces pulled
(b) Dress:—yes or no; Hepworths, Marks   1 2 3 4 5 6
    and Sparks; Jaeger; or Austin Reed
(c) Courtesy:—buys drinks for boss;   1 2 3 4 5 6
    compliments boss's wife; drives older
    car than boss
(d) Fitness:—can handle 18 holes before   1 2 3 4 5 6
    drinks at 11.00 am; can't do above;
    uses lift; travels by Southern Region
(e) Poise:—ability to hold drink; threw up   1 2 3 4 5 6
    at office party.

SOCIAL INTERACTION
(a) Participation in social activities:—who's   1 2 3 4 5 6
    he knocking off in the typing pool; are
    you jealous; does he stand a cat in
    hell's chance with the boss's daughter?
(b) Participation in local affairs:—does he/   1 2 3 4 5 6
    she have a criminal record; does this
    have any bearing on his/her work?
    wife-swapping; gossip-monger
(c) Ability to mix with people:—   1 2 3 4 5 6
    smooth-talking; socially inadequate;
    always plastered
(d) Attitudes with other people:—fascist;   1 2 3 4 5 6
    'liberal'; agrees with management;
    enjoys canteen food; (if male) does *not*
    lust after managing director's secretary.

PSYCHOLOGICAL EQUILIBRIUM SITUATION
(a) Reaction to stress:—total panic; the   1 2 3 4 5 6
    bottle; iron resolve; Valium
(b) General competence:—supreme;   1 2 3 4 5 6
    average; hopeless
(c) Degree of personal motivation at   1 2 3 4 5 6
    work:—(more degrees, less motivation)
(d) Childhood, adolescence and family   1 2 3 4 5 6
    background:—deprived; depraved;
    bourgeois; delinquent; Oedipus
    complex; chorister; brownie; listened
    to Uncle Mac; believed in Father
    Christmas; still believes in Father
    Christmas

LEADERSHIP
(a) Experience of leadership:—if employee   1 2 3 4 5 6
    works immediately beneath you, how
    good are you; how often have you
    been absent leaving employee to hold
    the baby; how disastrous was this; if
    not disastrous, how come you're still
    with us?
(b) Leadership motivation:—power-crazy;   1 2 3 4 5 6
    needs money to support mistress; will
    soon need money to pay alimony;
    wants a worker's state; wants change
    of office/car; needs promotion to get
    out of your hair; has nice legs which
    are wasted in . . . . at present.

MATURITY
(a) Senile; middle-aged (10 years older   1 2 3 4 5 6
    than you); precocious; one foot in the
    grave; one foot in the pram
(b) Personal drive:—best average distance   1 2 3 4 5 6
    over par four hole; wind direction;
    type of club used. (Nothing lower than
    '3' need be entered)
(c) Responsibility:—easy to blame; can be   1 2 3 4 5 6
    pinned down; slimy operator; obvious
    scapegoat; number of cock-ups in last
    twelve months

As every good personnel officer knows, when it comes to recruiting it pays to advertise ...

WANTED –
A FIRST CLASS MALE WAITRESS
ONLY QUALIFIED PERSONS CONSIDERED

WANTED – Part-time hotel receptionist and telephone operator (small broad). Apply Hotel Nicosia.

Cordon Bleu cook required for government department dining room. Good salary, excellent working conditions, bonuses, plus luncheon vouchers.

Unusual opportunity for biscuit salesman with a modern institution; Must have at least 2 years experience within last 6 months or do not apply.

Gentlemen required, knowledge of shorthand absolutely essential though not necessary.

TWO BUSINESS LADIES REQUIRE SLEEPING PARTNER FOR BEAUTY SALON

WANTED - Some additional female technicians at the fast-expanding Charles River Breeding Laboratory

---

Woman wanted to run up curtains.

Receptionist -telephonist required. -Must be prepared to work very occasional Saturday mornings (often).

WANTED - Cigarette makers (female) round and flat.

Revlon Ltd. require a SENIOR BEAUTY ADVISOR for a York store. Applicants should be mature cowmen.

Tea Room Attendant required. Knowledge of first aid essential.

Lady required for six hours work per week to clean small officers at Station Road, Witney.

LADIES! We are looking for caféteria insistants to work in our modern caféteria in the Grove Road Area. Successful applicants will be asked to work occasially.

Gravedigger's assistant wanted. Must be dead keen.

Woman required for looking over fixed bats and cranks in warehouse.

The organisation of this place is like a septic tank— Only the really big lumps rise to the top!

ONLY THE MEDIOCRE WORKER IS ALWAYS AT HIS BEST.

Hell knows no fury like a planner scorned.

Make sure brain is engaged before putting mouth in gear.

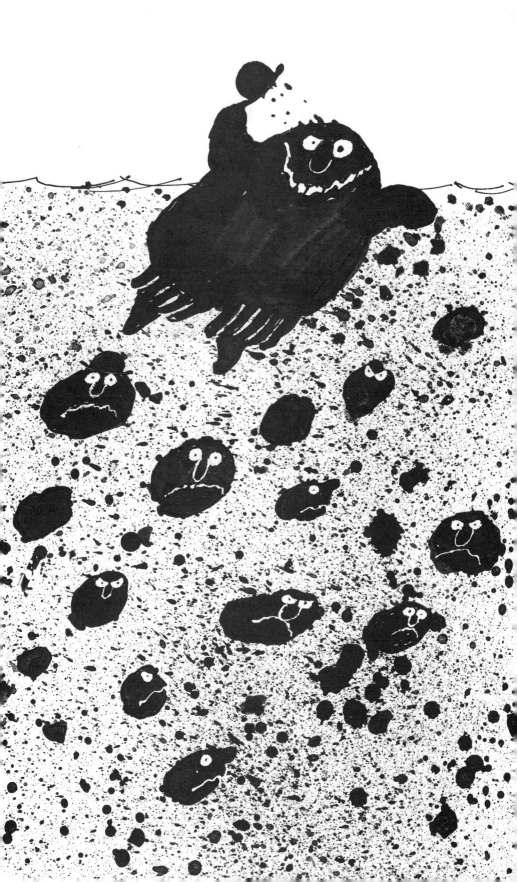

HOW TO BE A TROUBLE SHOOTER

If you want to be a successful trouble-shooter, these are the rules. Read on ...

(a) Profess not to have *the* answer. This lets you out of having *any* answer.

(b) Say that we must not move too rapidly. This avoids the need of getting started.

(c) For every proposal set up an opposite and conclude that the 'middle ground' (no motion whatever) represents the wisest course of action.

(d) Point out that any attempt to reach a conclusion is only a futile 'quest for certainty'. Doubt and uncertainty promote growth.

(e) When in a tight place say something that the group cannot understand.

(f) Argue that the problem 'cannot be separated' from other problems; therefore no problem can be solved until all other problems are solved.

(g) Point out that those who see the problem do so by virtue of personality traits, e.g. they are unhappy and transfer their dissatisfaction to the area under discussion.

(h) Ask what is meant by the question. When it is clarified there will be no time left for the answer.

(i) Retreat from the problem into endless discussion of various techniques for approaching it.

(j) Retreat into analogies and discuss them until everyone has forgotten the original problem.

(k) Point out that some of the greatest minds have struggled with the problem, implying that it does us credit to have thought of it.

(l) Be thankful for the problem. It has stimulated our best thinking and has, therefore, contributed to our growth. It (the problem) should get a medal.

HAPPINESS CAN'T BUY MONEY

I like being miserably rich!

othing vouchered, nothing gained.

NEY IS THE
OT OF ALL
IL...AND
MAN
EEDS ROOTS

BE POLITE TO EVERYBODY UNTIL YOU MAKE YOUR FIRST MILLION —AFTER THAT, EVERYBODY WILL BE POLITE TO YOU!

The man who can smile when things go wrong has thought of the person he can blame it on.

HOW TO MASTER THE LANGUAGE OF BUSINESS

The successful operator in the modern world of business
needs to have a feeling for poetry ...

I had a little document,
As pure as driven snow,
Yet everywhere that paper went,
It wandered to and fro.

I thought that people gladly
And swiftly would concur,
But while I waited sadly,
They'd cavil and demur.

Some thought the paper much too short;
Others much too long.
Some thought the language much too weak;
Others much too strong.

So by the time that document came dawdling back my way
It made no difference where it went –
The issue was passé!

If you have no natural flair for language don't despair, the Executive Loquaculator is here ...

It has come to our attention that certain senior personnel have been singularly lacking in the modern-as-tomorrow, authoritative, contract-winning terminology that this company needs to maintain its place in our market sector. Accordingly the Board has undertaken an in-depth survey to provide all management and senior grades with an easy-to-use, fact-fudging instrument which will provide three words, where, until now, a pause has had to suffice.

By selecting any word from each of the three columns it is hoped that the users will be able to sharpen up their language while successfully glossing over any embarrassing details that they may be forced to expose from time to time.

The choice is almost endless – USE IT.

1	Permanent	Concordant	Interdependence
2	Positivistic	Digital	Structure
3	Bilateral	Imitative	Polarity
4	Partial	Discrepant	Specification
5	Flanking	Recessive	Implication
6	Divergent	Expansive	Affinity
7	Quantitative	Decentralized	Potency
8	Integrated	Contributory	Motivation
9	Gradual	Incremental	Flexibility
10	Ultimative	Monitored	Factionalism
11	Intransigent	Innovative	Diffusion
12	Responsive	Convergent	Escalation
13	Differentiated	Dynamic	Feasibility
14	Nonfragmenting	Logistical	Periodicity
15	Predicative	Conglomerate	Consistency
16	Temporal	Differential	Accumulation
17	Synchronized	Aggregating	Transcendence
18	Structural	Eliminative	Solidification
19	Representative	Diversifying	Competence
20	Societal	Homogeneous	Adaptation
21	Obsolete	Universal	Capability
22	Systematized	Fluctuating	Projection
23	Parallel	Simulated	Extension
24	Dialectical	Identifying	Mobility
25	Compatible	Usurpative	Expectancy
26	Gradual	Transitional	Phase
27	Multilateral	Culminating	Concept
28	Optional	Complementary	Classification
29	Indicative	Deteriorative	Plasticity
30	Functional	Elongating	Mobility
31	Reversibile	Prior	Eventuality
32	Determinative	Exponential	Extrapolation
33	Global	Allocated	Transparency
34	Total	Participatory	Efficiency
35	Substantial	Restrictive	Time phase
36	Balanced	Transfigurative	Options
37	Concentrated	Programmed	Equivalence
38	Synchronous	Reciprocal	Projection
39	contradictory	Organizational	Vacancy
40	Interfractional	Uniform	Programming
41	Distributive	Progressive	Permanence
42	Inductive	Unilateral	Synthesis
43	Coherent	Management	Application
44	Proliferative	Co-operative	Sufficiency
45	Compatible	Coincidental	Finality
46	Ameliorating	Exemplificatory	Discontinuity
47	Descriptive	Erupting	Cancellation
48	Ambivalent	Component	Denudation
49	Existential	Obstructive	Epigenesis
50	Coincidental	Illusory	Disparity

EXECUTIVE VOCABULARY

Understanding what's *really* being said.

Automatic	Can't repair it yourself.
Bank	Institution which will lend you an umbrella and demand its return as soon as it rains.
Blackleg	Eccentric who treats the right to work as if it was for real.
Boss	Relatively low-cost, automatic device installed by senior management to spy on work force.
Career defence	Cover your backside.
Cash	The working man's credit card.
Coffee break	Opportunity to buy cup of coffee for under 20p.
Conference	Place where conversation is substituted for the dreariness of labour and the loneliness of thought. – A meeting of the bored.
Consultant	Person who borrows your watch to tell you the time before walking off with the watch. – Unemployed practitioner.
Coordinator	The person who has a desk between two expediters.
Discussion	General pooling of ignorance.
Expedite	To confound confusion with commotion.
Good idea	One your boss is convinced he/she thought of first.
Industrial tribunal	Welfare agency from which workers may collect bonuses for being sacked.

In conference	Never available when you want him/her.
In due course	Never.
Keen worker	One that looks for something to occupy his/her time after he/she has been given a job.
Living wage	Sum covering broad financial spectrum governed by whether you're giving or receiving.
Memorandum	Something written, not to inform the reader but to protect the writer.
Moderate	One who makes enemies left and right.
Nationalized industry	One that expands by contracting debt.
Occupational hazard	Having to work occasionally.
Policy	Convenient shield offering shelter in case of disaster or enquiry.
Programme	Any assignment that cannot be dealt with by one phone call.
Recession	When your neighbour loses his job (not to be confused with 'depression' – when you lose yours)
Rich man	Poor man with money.
Slogan	Ancient substitute for argument or fact.

Sources

Reliable source	The person you just met.
Informed source	The person who told the person you just met.
Unimpeachable source	The person who started the rumour in the first place.
The very best authority	Your own guesswork.
Steady worker	One up from motionless worker.
Taxpayer	Person who doesn't need to take a Civil Service exam to work for the Government.
Top priority	It's idiotic, but the boss wants it.

PART TWO: PHRASES

Correct within an order of magnitude	Wrong
It is clear that much additional work will be required before a complete understanding ...	I haven't a clue
Let's take a survey	We need more time to think of an answer
It might be argued that ...	I have such a good answer to this objection that I shall now raise it
The most reliable values are those of Jones	He trained under me
These results will be reported at a later date	I might possibly get round to it sometime
For your consideration	You hold the bag for a while
Three of these samples were chosen for detailed study	The results on the others didn't make sense and were ignored
... accidentally stained during mounting	... dropped on the floor
... handled with extreme care throughout the experiments	... nearly dropped on the floor
Competition elimination	Screw your buddies
Developed after years of intensive research	Discovered by accident
Typical results are shown	The best results are shown
Give us the benefit of your wide experience in this field	We don't mind listening to you since we've already decided what course to follow

It is hoped that this work will stimulate further investigation in this field	This report isn't up to much, but neither is any of the other work on this miserable subject
Let's get together on this	I reckon you're as confused as I am
Take under advisement	Ignore and hope everyone will forget it
Approved, subject to comment	Redraft the damned thing
Although some detail has been lost in reproduction, it is clear from the original micrograph	It is impossible to tell a thing from the micrograph
Give someone the picture, to	To make a long, confused and inaccurate statement to a newcomer
Verbal containment	Shut your mouth
Under active consideration	We're searching the files for it
Under consideration	Never heard of it
The agreement with the predicted curve	
is excellent	Fair
... good	Poor
... satisfactory	Doubtful
... fair	Imaginary
... is in the process	... is so wrapped up in red tape that any progress is hopeless
We will advise you in due course	If we can work it out, we'll be in touch

For examples of the language of business at its most eloquent, poetic and powerful, read on. Every quotation is guaranteed genuine ...

From a patent application:
Apparatus from removing casings from sausages and the like (US Patent No. 2,672,646)

In a sausage-skinning machine, means for rotating a sausage about its longitudinal axis, means for simultaneously holding a part of the skin against rotative movement with the sausage to cause said skin to be torn off said sausage circumferentially, and means for simultaneously moving said sausage endwise with respect to said holding means, said rotating, holding and moving means being operatively related to one another to cause said skin to be torn off and stripped from the sausage helically.

From the US Revenue Act 1940:
Component corporations of component corporations – If a corporation is a component corporation of an acquiring corporation, under subsection (b) or under this subsection, it shall (except for the purpose of section 742d and section 743a) also be a component corporation of the corporation of which such acquiring corporation is a component corporation.

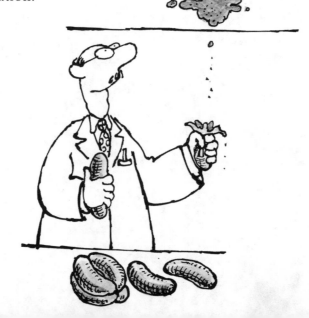

From the house magazine of an American research laboratory:
'Any employee whose current salary rate exceeds the new top of the salary range for his or her classification will not be eligible for the general increase unless the new top of the salary range for his or her classification exceeds the employee's current salary rate.'

From the National Insurance Act 1959:
'For the purpose of this Part of the Schedule a person over pensionable age, not being an insured person, shall be treated as an insured person if he would be an insured person were he under pensionable age and would be an employed person were he an insured person.'

From the minutes of evidence taken by a Royal Commission on the Civil Service:
'What I have said has demonstrated that it is very difficult to find an answer to that question, but if I were pressed for an answer I would say that, so far as we can see, taking it rather by and large, taking one time with another, and taking the average of Departments, it is probable that there would not be found to be very much in it either way.'

*From the Occupational Safety and Health Administration
Rulebook – defining an exit as:*
'... that portion of a means of egress which is separated
from all other spaces of the building or structure by
construction or equipment as required in this subpart to
provide a protected way of travel to the exit discharge.'

and subsequently defining a 'means of egress' as:
'... a continuous and unobstructed way of exit travel from
any point in a building or structure to a public way and
consists of three separate and distinct parts: the way of exit
access, the exit and the way of exit discharge.'

From an Australian circular on employment:
The admission of domestic workers from abroad was
confined to female applicants. This restriction has been
relaxed. The term 'girl' now stands
for any type of applicant regardless
of sex.

From a form issued to employers by the Department of Employment:
'Separate departments of the same premises are treated as separate premises for this purpose where separate branches of work which are commonly carried on in separate premises are carried on in separate departments on the same premises.'

From a letter sent out by the Department of Employment:
'Unemployment benefit is not payable in respect of the dates quoted which cannot be treated as days of unemployment on the ground that the claimant notwithstanding that this employment has terminated received, by way of compensation for the loss of the remuneration which he would have received for that day each of those days if the unemployment had not been terminated, payment of an amount which exceeds the amount arrived at by deducting the standard daily rate of unemployment benefit from two-thirds of the remuneration lost in respect of that day each of those days.'

From a Treasury circular:
In conformity with a Treasury order which has just been issued, official correspondence should not refer to the 'devaluation of the £'. Some such phrase as 'the change in the dollar rate' should be used instead.

From a report of Water Softening Sub-Committee of the Central Advisory Committee:
'We do suggest, within very wide limits, washing a desirable habit.'

From a Department of Trade bulletin:
Leave Regulations – Section 3. When an employee absent from duty on account of illness dies without making application for advanced sick leave, the fact of death is sufficient to show a 'serious disability' and to dispense with the requirement of a formal application and a medical certificate.

From a BBC memorandum:
Distinguish between an Extra and a Walk-on:
(1)   A 'policeman' standing at the corner of a street, alone, but not doing anything in particular, would be an Extra. If he was called upon to do anything specific to the action of a drama he becomes a Walk-on I; if he speaks he is a Walk-on II.
(2)   A 'barman' seen in long-shot busying himself in normal barman work would be an extra; if he serves a pint to a leading character on cue he becomes a Walk-on I; if he speaks a few unimportant words, he becomes a Walk-on II.
(3)   A 'gardener' alone in a long-shot sweeping a drive would be an Extra; if he is seen in close-up grimacing, he becomes a Walk-on II.

From the pen of one of the true Bards of Bureaucracy:

THE INGRATITUDES

Cursed are the poor in spirit: for they never get a rise.
Cursed are they that moan: for they shall never be
comforted.
Cursed are the meek: for they shall accept the
management's offer.
Cursed are they which do hunger and thirst after canteen
lunches: for all their complaints are just filed.
Cursed are the careful: for all they get are cares.
Cursed are the pure in heart: for they shall see through the
rest of us.
Cursed are the peace-makers: for they shall be called scabs.
Cursed are they who are persecuted for righteousness' sake:
for theirs is the dole queue.
Cursed are ye, when men shall revile you, and persecute
you, and shall say all manner of evil against you falsely for
the strike's sake.
Mourn, and be exceeding sad: for meagre is your reward in
compensation: for so persecuted they the shop stewards
who worked for you.

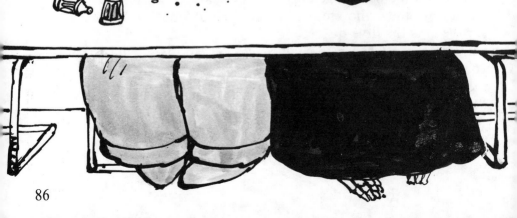

It was felt by the Luncheon Club Committee that although Crême Caramel was on the menu more frequently after the previous meeting, it had tended to drop off recently.

SAVE THE WHALE -DON'T EAT HERE!

OFFICE USE ONLY
May also be used for coats.

taff should empty
e tea-pots and then
and upside down
n tea trays.

HOW TO MASTER DESK ARCHERY

For those moments of inactivity or intense frustration when hands stray idly through desk drawers and usually come to rest on rubber bands, paper clips, bottles of ink, empty gin bottles, which alone serve no useful purpose, DESK ARCHERY offers an entertaining, skilful and demanding activity that will take you out of yourself and prevent you from pushing your boss down the lift-shaft or falling asleep over your desk out of sheer boredom.

CHOOSE YOUR WEAPONS

For **DESK ARCHERY** all you will need are two raised fingers, or possibly one raised finger and one raised thumb, and three rubber bands.

The rubber bands are looped together to produce one long rubber band, which is then attached to the two raised digits to form a sling.

Projectiles may take many forms – lumps of Blu-tac; staples; pencils; folded strips of paper; or lumps of sugar. The only deciding factor in choosing your weapon is that it should make a mark on the target. (Strips of paper dipped in ink are usually the most popular – though you need to develop a good aim before getting too carried away.)

The game can be played individually to better a personal score, or between two or more players to decide who buys the first round/first asks for a rise/makes the next pot of tea.

In the absence of a suitable target, other than office personnel, this page has proved very successful in the limited space available to most competitors.

FOOLS RUSH IN WHERE
FOOLS HAVE BEEN BEFORE!

Experience is what you get when
you failed to get what you wanted.

My boss is Irish.
He's made me an
offer I can't understand.

oil is thicker than blood !

AN OPTIMIST IS SOMEONE WHO'S NEVER HAD MUCH EXPERIENCE.

The man who knows 'how' will never be without a job. The man who knows 'why' will always be his boss.

HOW TO SUCCEED IN BUSINESS WITHOUT DOING A THING

You too can create a professional paradise, your own Garden of Eden at the office, your own Heaven on the shop-floor. If only you know how to set about it, a workers' wonderland is yours ...

OFFICE YOU-TOPIA

In spite of what people say to the contrary there's only one person that matters in your office – you. If you want to cock things up, there's very little anyone else can do about it, and if they try, there's the Industrial Tribunal to see you right. However, careful planning and the creation of the right impression can provide a convincing camouflage at work that will let you get on with life, without being overburdened by other distractions between nine and five. It's all a matter of strategy.

Work Planning

This always looks good. It doesn't require much effort and it certainly won't require any real work. Keenies plan their work by the day, the week and the month, so do the same. Simply list all the outstanding things you failed to do last week, last month and yesterday and put them down in one of those flashy desk diaries that multinationals give away at Christmas. Leave this lying around open at the relevant day and you shouldn't be too bothered with people finding things for you to do. Remember that even the best plans can be upset by emergencies. Flexibility is the name of the game and you should allow gaps in each schedule to accommodate: rail strikes; lengthy negotiations with the pretty clerk in charge of the stationery cupboard; tea-break consultations; visits to the bookies to see what odds they're offering on Kerry Packer buying British Leyland in order to get his hands on Lord's. Don't forget to cross off items as time passes – they can always be entered again later under another name.

Reference Books

As well as the diary, mentioned above, you'll find a personal reference book an invaluable aid. This can be used for recording such details as how much coffee everyone else drinks and whether they're paying their fair share. You can use it for keeping a note of the boss's punctuality, a useful ploy when you're being hauled over the carpet for being late yourself. Names and telephone numbers need somewhere to go, too; this little book is the obvious place.

There are certain general reference books that should be at hand, too. *The Good Food Guide*, and the latest *Real Ale Guide* are obviously essential, but others have their uses:

Railway Timetables	Good for a laugh and handy for delaying unwelcome visitors.
Michelin Guides	For planning business trips abroad.
The Sporting Life	For keeping abreast of the market.
The Times	For the crossword.
The Sun	For keeping abreast of the market.

Essential Office Equipment

Apart from the kettle, the bottle opener and the corkscrew, which should be to the office what a lift is to a lift-shaft, the following articles are frequently found in well appointed offices (any office without the above mentioned can probably be done under the Health and Safety at Work Act);

Stapling machine and staples	For Desk Archery
Perforator (punch)	For creative work with paper.
Scissors	For further creative work with paper; mending plugs; running repairs to work clothes.
Sellotape	For repairing window cracks; silencing office bores; repairing coffee cups; resealing confidential mail steamed open over kettle.
Ash tray	For feeding office cat; collecting beer money; drawing lots for any major decision (e.g. who buys first round).
Telex pads	For notes; Desk Archery; messages on the strange machine that rattles out messages from time to time.
Paper clips, rubber bands	For Desk Archery.
Blu-tac	For mounting page 3; for sticking under adversary's desk like old chewing gum; for plugging leaks in kettle, or anything else; for Desk Archery.

Dress and Grooming

Care should be taken over one's appearance at work.
The men should try to give the impression of genteel
poverty. Sharp suits, silk ties, Russell and Bromley
shoes, cashmere coats do nothing, if you want a rise,
except make your boss envious. Dress for the office
as you would if you were appearing in court in a
divorce case and wanted to dodge paying through the
nose. Hair, if you still have any, should be cared for
with an eye to the typing pool. If you're in the typing
pool it should be cared for with an eye to the Director
of Finance, or if he's beyond the pale, his son. If you
give as much attention dressing for the office as you
would to a party, fancy-dress or otherwise, you will
always be certain of gaining the right attention.

Posture

Posture is never more important in the office than after lunch. The temptation to slump against the wall of the lift, clutching onto the ventilator grill, must be resisted at all costs; you never know who may be waiting to get in when the doors open on your floor. At your desk it's as well to sit as upright as you can, making sure that your head is perpendicular to your centre of gravity. When walking about the office, walk straight and positively until you're out of the door. If you're in doubt about making it in a straight line, try to go out with a friend who can steer you in the right direction.

Office Communication and Correspondence

It can't all be left to machines and sometimes it can't be left to other people either. So when you're forced into putting pen to paper, or mouth to microphone remember the rules:

1. Don't use no double negatives.
2. Make each pronoun agree with their antecedent.
3. Join clauses good, like a conjunction should.
4. About them sentence fragments.
5. When dangling, watch your particles.
6. Verbs has to agree with their subject.
7. Just between you and I, case are important to.
8. Don't write run-on sentences they are hard to read.
9. Don't use commas, which aren't necessary.
10. Try to not oversplit infinitives.

WHEN IN DOUBT, SMILE
—IT ALWAYS MAKES PEOPLE
WONDER WHAT YOU'RE THINKING.

Success is a matter of luck — just ask any failure!

WHEN IN CHARGE, PONDER.
WHEN IN TROUBLE, DELEGATE

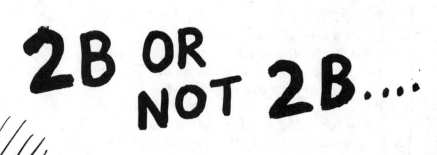

2B OR NOT 2B....

Give more than they ask for.
More is less, but it looks like more.

A rolling stone angers his boss.

GENIUS IS 10% INSPIRATION
AND 50% CAPITAL GAINS.

HOW TO SUCCEED IN BUSINESS
BY TRYING DESPERATELY HARD

ROBBIN'S RULES OF MARKETING

1. Your share of the market is really lower than you think.
2. Never delay the end of a meeting or the beginning of a cocktail hour.
3. The combined market position goals of all competitors always totals at least 150 per cent.
4. The existence of a market does not always ensure the existence of a customer.
5. Strategies develop most easily from big backlogs.
6. Beware of alleged needs that have no real market.
7. The worth of a thing is what it will bring.
8. Low price and long shipment will win over high price and short shipment.
9. Umbrella pricing encourages noncompetitive costs.
10. The competition really can have lower prices.
11. If you can't get the whole job, settle for part of it.
12. The number of competitors never decline.
13. Secret negotiations are usually neither.
14. A good presentation has as many questions as answers.

15. If the customer wants vanilla, give him vanilla.
16. If the customer buys lunch, you've lost the order.
17. Unless constantly nurtured, nothing is as short-lived as a good customer.
18. No matter how good the deal, the customer is always sceptical.

1. To study a subject best, understand it thoroughly before you start.
2. Always keep a record of data. It indicates you've been working.
3. Always draw your curves, then plot the reading.
4. In case of doubt, make it sound convincing.
5. Experiments should be reproducible. They should all fail in the same way.
6. Do not believe in miracles. Rely on them.
7. If an experiment works, something has gone wrong.
8. No matter what result is anticipated, there will always be someone eager (a) to misinterpret it, (b) fake it, or (c) believe it happened to his own pet theory.
9. In any collection of data, the figure most obviously correct, beyond all need of checking, is the mistake.
    Corollary 1: No one whom you ask for help will see it.
    Corollary 2: Everyone who stops by with unsought advice will see it immediately.
10. Once a job is fouled up, anything done to improve it only makes it worse.
11. Science is truth – don't be misled by facts.

1. He who gets too big for his britches gets exposed in the end.
2. Staying afloat in management is easier if you don't make big waves.
3. The only people making money these days are the ones who sell computer paper.
4. If you don't have problems, you wouldn't need people around to help solve them. Conversely, if you didn't have people around, maybe you wouldn't have problems.
5. Nothing motivates a man more than to see his boss putting in an honest day's work.
6. Bosses are so busy delegating jobs, they have no time to do any work.
7. When someone else blows their horn, it sounds like a Cadillac. When *you* toot, it sounds like a Volkswagen.
8. People who mind their business succeed because they have so little competition.
9. You can tell some people aren't afraid of work by the way they fight it.

SPARK'S TEN RULES FOR THE PROJECT MANAGER

1. Strive to look tremendously important.
2. Attempt to be seen with important people.
3. Speak with authority; however, only expound on the obvious and proven facts.
4. Don't engage in arguments, but if cornered, ask an irrelevant question and lean back with a satisfied grin while your opponent tries to figure out what's going on – then quickly change the subject.
5. Listen intently while others are arguing the problem. Pounce on a trite statement and bury them with it.
6. If a subordinate asks you a pertinent question, look at him as if he had lost his senses. When he looks down, paraphrase the question back at him.
7. Obtain a brilliant assignment, but keep out of sight and out of the limelight.
8. Walk at a fast pace when out of the office – this keeps questions from subordinates and superiors at a minimum.
9. Always keep the office door closed. This puts visitors on the defensive and also makes it look as if you are always in an important conference.
10. Give all orders verbally. Never write anything down that might be used in evidence against you.

DECISION MAKING

1) **If** you must make a decision, delay it.

2) **If** you can authorise someone else to avoid a decision, do so.

3) **If** you can form a committee, have them avoid a decision.

4) **If** you can otherwise avoid a decision, avoid it immediately.

THOSE WHO THINK THEY KNOW IT ALL UPSET THOSE OF US THAT DO!

Necessity is the mother of convention.

IT'S COMPANY POLICY —WORK HARD OR LOOK GOOD IN A TIGHT SWEATER!

The wages of sin vary considerably.

HOW TO BE AN INTERNATIONAL EXECUTIVE

MASTER THE LANGUAGES OF INTERNATIONAL BUSINESS . . .

THE BUSINESSMAN ABROAD: A MULTINATIONAL PHRASE BOOK

à bientôt	just a drop
abito	some, a piece of
ab imo	it's his
achtung	I've got a sore mouth
actif	keen
action préférentielle	nepotism
à fond	source of money
ahorro	boss's personal assistant
aide de camp	gay p.a.
à la carte	served from the trolley
amende honorable	proper (decent) repair to clothing
analyse du chemin critique	how to get back to the office after 'business' lunch

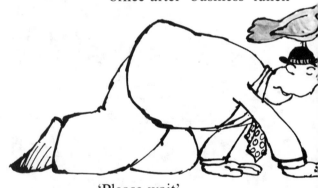

Angebot	'Please wait'
Anlage	'Skol, please'
apenas	joy, pleasure (often the source of)
apéritif	dentures
artichaut	sneeze
Aussicht	domestic illness
Autofahrt	backfire
avant-garde	chastity belt

108

bagatelle	talkative woman
baroque	hiccup in cash flow
battre le pavé	thump the pavement
bénéfices d'exploitation	backhander
bien	French vegetable
billet	academic qualification
bord de la route	soliciting hitchhiker
brouhaha	French joy of cooking
Brottosozialprodukt	juvenile delinquent

ça ne fait rien	good weather
capuccino	small hat
cercle privé	lavatory seat
c'est magnifique	it's huge, enormous
château	French small talk
chômage	respect shown to boss
compota, compôte	left-overs
coq d'or	entry to Gents
cortège	weekend retreat
cum priviligio	he had the honour of her company

damnosa	inquisitive
déjeuner	to travel
déjâ vu	boo!
de mal en pis	'Where's the …?'

déshabiller	to kick the habit
disponsibilités	passing the buck
Elite	match
émeraudes	piles
émigré	violent headache
émission d'actions gratuites	slush fund

en arrière	suppository
en gros	overweight
épices	business entertaining
esprit de corps	liquor served in service messes
extrados	more please
fabrication	annual report
faggotto	cigarette
farci	result of excessive stuffing with food
faux pas	don't do it
fiasco	Italian wine bottle
flèche	skin
(à) forte intensité de main	a bunch of fives
frais généraux	bonuses
fruits de mer	sea weed
gendarme	the strong arm of the law
gestion de stock	quality control (catering)
Gewinnspanne	aircraft tool
grand prix	boast
Grosshandel	clumsy
Gurke	pardon
hasta la vista	you have nice views
Haushalt	front door
heures supplementaires	overmanning in typing pool
homme d'affaires	busy man; gigolo
homo sapiens	consenting adult
hors concours	horse chestnut
hors de combat	camp followers
horloge	house of low repute

In toto	nail
infra dig	archaeologist
in statu pupillari	contact lens
inter alia	Italian internal flights
intermezzo	period between meals
in vino veritas	'there is a worm in my wine'

jeu d'esprit	piss up
jus divinum	wine
karat	vegetable like an orange turnip
kip	chicken
kipper	chick
laissez-faire	secretary to whom job satisfaction has little to do with shorthand and typing
Lagerkontrolle	barman
lampone	raspberry
legato	foot
libido	bathroom fitting
libretto	type of sandal
lingua franca	laying it on the line
'L'état c'est moi'	'I am in a state'
lieu	(in lieu), engaged
Lockartikel	key

maladie	French distraction
mal de mer	battered baby
marge bénéficiaire	canteen cost-cutting propaganda
marché à terme	lift out of order
marque de fabrique	incontinence
matières brutes	industrial relations
ménage à trois	to share the burden
negligé	cause of distraction; careless
n'importe	trade barrier
noblesse oblige	it's too late to repent
non compos mentis	non-biodegradable
nota bene	potato
obiit	push off!
odium theologicum	incense
omphallus	large symbol
par excellence	professional golf handicap
pas de deux	father of twins
passé	the old man said
per annum	laxative
piano	shipping line
pis aller	gutter
pizzicato	Italian take-away
polonaise	hay fever
post-obitum	earth re-entry
presto	tight (shoe)
prévisions	canteen orders

quod erat demonstrandum	there are four mistakes
rentier	payment to landlord
sang froid	black pudding
savoir faire	to know 'a good thing'
semper paratus	once a parrot, always a parrot
son et lumière	'boy, you're lit up!'
sotto voce	slurred speech
sub poena	(as above) under the piano
table d'hôte	hot dish
tant pis	Auntie's had too much

tartine	sweet little French waitress
terra cotta	clinophobia
terra firma	fear of business organizations
terra incognita	fear of the unknown
tertium quid	3,000 new pence
tour de force	inspection
tour de main	palmistry
tout de suite	all the pudding
vidi, vici, veni	'I saw, I conquered, I came'. See 'wanderlust'
vis-à-vis	to return the insult
voltarsi	leap-frog

Wanderlust	see: 'bord de la route'
Zweifellos	a couple of chaps

And know who to call when you need them ...

INTERNATIONAL TELEPHONE DIRECTORY

Don't waste time wading through other directories only
to make dud calls. Go straight to the top and main-line
it where it counts! (Area codes not provided):

President Reagan   Washington D.C. 456–2573
President Brehzhnev   Moscow 206–25–11
Henry Ford   Dearborn 322–3000
Euthanasia Education
   Council, Inc.   New York 246–6962

Horoscopes	New York 936–5950/6262
Salvation Army Alcohol	
and Drug Addiction	
Centre	Sydney 272–2322
Ambulance Service	Bangkok 13
Musée des Beaux Arts	Beirut 2–52–85
NASA	Washington D.C. 755–8364
Worldwide Rent-a-Car	Sharjah 355547
Dial-an-angel	Sydney 467–1511
Credit Suisse	Zurich 215–1111
Oil Can Harry's	Vancouver 683–7306
St. George Brewery	Addis Ababa 47295
North Pizza Pantry	Tehran 285765
International Casino	Nairobi 56000

Windsor Castle	Windsor 68286
Playboy Enterprises Inc.	Chicago 751–8000
Magistrate's Office	Soweto 825–1061
Christian Dior	Paris 359–83–72
Gucci	Los Angeles 278–3451
Pinkerton's, Inc.	New York 285–4860
Guyana Distilleries Ltd.	Georgetown 66171
British Embassy	Ulan Bator 51033/4
Dial-a-Girl	Johannesburg 23–9547
Colt Fire-arms	Hartford 278–8550
Gstaad Golf Course	Gstaad 42636
Ministry of Education	Zomba 611
'La Poms' (hairdresser)	Auckland 65–777
Air & Sea Rescue	Bahamas 2–3877
Sony Corporation	Tokyo 448–2111
Watergate	Washington D.C. 965–2300
Raffles Hotel	Singapore 328041
Cartier Inc.	New York 753–0111
Comdates Computer Service	San Francisco 391–8181
Warner Brothers Inc.	Burbank 845–6000
Acropolis	Athens 3236–665
Sunset Club	Lima 22–9874
Texaco, Inc.	White Plains 253–4000
Teatro alla Scala	Milan 8879
Topkapi Palace	Istanbul 28–35–47
Wayside Chapel Crisis Centre	Sydney 33–4251
Committee for the Scientific Investigation of Claims of the Paranormal	Buffalo 837–0306

Penthouse Club	Copenhagen 14–35–35
Ting Li Kwan Restaurant	Peking 281–936
The Raja of Perlis	Perlis 7552211
Central Intelligence Agency	Washington D.C. 351–1100
Omaha Grain Exchange	Omaha 341–6733
Dubai Broadcasting	Dubai 470255
Professional Rodeo Cowboys Association	Denver 455–3270
Champagne J. Bollinger SA	Reims 50–12–34
Kaziranga Wildlife Sanctuary	Kaziranga 3

SUCCESS IS MAKING MORE MONEY TO PAY THE TAXES YOU WOULDN'T HAVE TO PAY IF YOU DIDN'T MAKE SO MUCH MONEY

off the top of the head ideas are like dandruff — small and flaky!

DESIGN DEPARTMENT

MANY HANDS
WANT LIGHT WORK

They are not long,
   the Days of Whine and Rises.

Money isn't everything
It isn't even enough!

THEY TOLD HIM THE JOB
            COULDN'T BE DONE;

HE ROLLED UP HIS SLEEVES
            AND SET TO IT.

HE TACKLED THE JOB
            THAT COULDN'T BE DONE;

—AND HE COULDN'T DO IT!

HOW TO LIVE ON YOUR SALARY

Be philosophic about it ... you can't.

ON THEIR MEANNESS
(*With acknowledgement to J. Milton*)

When I consider how my time is spent,
Ere half my days, working fiddles on the side,
And that one talent for which so hard I tried,
Lodged with me useless, my hours hell bent
To appease therewith my bank manager and present
A black account, lest he return post chide,
Doth the top brass expect slave-labour, pay increases
    denied,
I fondly ask; but a memo to prevent
That murmur, soon replies, this firm doth not need
Either men's brains or their own gifts, who best
Bear our workload, they serve us best, their state
Is humble. Executives on a whim may speed
Away to bask by sun-drenched oceans on American
    Express:
But increments for you, for the upturn must await.

And you must accept that the size of your salary merely reflects the hours you work ...

OUR WORKING SCHEDULE

Starting time	9.00 am
Morning Coffee Break	9.30–11.30 am
Lunch Hour	12.00–2.00 pm
Afternoon Tea Break	2.30–4.30 pm
Home Time	5.00 pm

The management has decided to introduce a more efficient and easily understood time-sheet. The time-sheet is designed for submission on a monthly basis but the firm has arranged for the data to be submitted at fortnightly intervals. In spite of the fact that data are submitted fortnightly, staff should complete time sheets each week.

Some time between starting and quitting time, without infringing on lunch periods, coffee breaks, rest periods, storytelling, ticket-selling, holiday planning, and the rehashing of yesterday's TV programme, we ask that each employee try to find some time for a work break.
This may seem radical, but it might aid steady employment, assure regular pay checks.

Spielman Chevrolet Company of New York.

NOTICE TO ALL EMPLOYEES

In view of the recently adopted 'personal productivity remuneration and increment contract' (PPRIC) you are reminded that your salary is your personal business, and should not be disclosed to anyone. Employees found revealing their PPRICs to other member of staff will be dealt with according to the agreed disciplinary procedure.

He who ploughs a straight furrow is probably in a rut

SOME PEOPLE ARE STILL WILLING TO DO AN HONEST DAY'S WORK, BUT THEY WANT A WEEK'S PAY FOR IT!

If you try You might If you don't You won't!

IF YOU CAN'T SEE THE BRIGHT SIDE — POLISH THE DULL SIDE

In this company all employees are completely dispensible — except when they want a day

The difference between this firm and a cactus plant is that the plant has the pricks on the outside

drink to make
other people
interesting.
RINK & THE WORLD DRINKS WITH YOU;
VOMIT & YOU VOMIT ALONE.
I USED TO BE A SCHIZOPHRENIC BUT NOW I'M LONELY.

The chances are that something of major importance will be happening at 9.00 am the morning after the binge – a board meeting; a crucial sales meeting; the signing of the contract. Whatever it is you're never in shape for it. Worse still, you've got to face the rest of the office. But if you can pull yourself together, retrieve your head and clear it, when everyone else is wishing they'd quietly disposed of theirs, you could score a few valuable status points. So the morning after should be spent wisely. A couple of hours can work miracles.

HANGOVER TIMETABLE

6.50 am.	Open eyes
6.55 am.	Focus eyes
7.00 am.	Reach for radio-alarm
7.01 am.	Turn off radio
7.10 am.	Rise and stagger to bathroom

7.15 am.	Clean teeth thoroughly
7.20 am.	Drink as much water as you can – then drink some more
7.30 am.	Drink glass of water with two seltzers
7.32 am.	Take shower, or bath if you can't stand up
7.50 am.	Shave
7.55 am.	Drink more water and clean teeth again
8.00 am.	Breakfast – porridge with salt and cream; cereals with plenty of milk and soft brown sugar; dry toast; scrambled eggs; whatever you reckon you can keep down. PLUS lots of hot, sweet tea or coffee.

8.20 am. Leave table and prepare morning's treat (you need something to pep you up by now)

8.25 am. Morning treat – whichever of the following you fancy, or can manage:
Sparkling wine (Champagne if you can afford it and don't mind the waste)
Fresh orange juice
Mixed in proportions of three to one
or,
2 tablespoons of scotch
3 tablespoons double cream
3 tablespoons honey
Shake (or stir if you can't take the noise) with ice and sip soothingly
or,
1 tablespoon of lemon juice
1 tablespoon of Worcestershire sauce
6 drops Tabasco
1 measure of Vodka (according to quantity of tomato juice)
Stir with ice

8.30 am. Leave for work with thermos of hot, sweet beverage to drink in private before facing the office

8.55 am. Clean teeth once more; wash face in cold water; drink contents of thermos; comb hair and straighten tie.

9.00 am. SOCK IT TO 'EM, BABY!

A WORKERS' PRAYER

Our gaffer who art a heathen,
Broken be thy name.
Thy receiver come.
Thy ruin done from Perth as far as Devon.
But give us till then our weekly bread.
And forgive us our secondary picketing,
As we forgive them that blackleg against us.
And lead us not into arbitration;
But deliver the gravy:
For thine is the Greek island,
The Rolls and the mistress,
Paid for by the sweat of
Our men.